By Craig Denison

Living Intentionally

Finding Meaning with a Modern Rule of Life

Denison Ministries
Dallas, Texas
www.denisonministries.org

Editing: Shayla Raquel
Illustration: Kathryn Burton
Book Design/Formatting: Matt Ravenelle

ISBN: 978-1-7357630-2-6

To those who have illuminated
the inner journey.
May we follow in your steps and forge new paths.

About First15

Spending consistent time alone with God can be a struggle. We're busier—and more stressed—than ever. But still, we know it's important to spend unhindered time with our Creator. We know we need to read his word, pray, and worship him.

First15 bridges the gap between desire and reality, helping you establish the rhythm of meaningful, daily experiences in God's presence. First15 answers the critical questions:

• Why should I spend time alone with God?
• How do I spend time alone with God?
• How do I get the most out of my time alone with God?
• How can I become more consistent in my time alone with God?

And by answering these questions through daily devotionals, we help people practice the rhythm of meeting with God while experiencing the incredible gift of his loving presence.

To learn more about First15, visit our website First15.org. The First15 devotional is also available on our mobile app, email, podcast, and website.

Contact: contact@first15.org
www.first15.org

"The plans of the diligent lead surely to abundance."

—Proverbs 21:5

Table of Contents

Unintentional Consequences

⚘

"One is not born into the world to do everything but to do something."

—Henry David Thoreau

Life Happens

Do you ever feel like most of your life just happens to you? As in, instead of choosing the things that fill your day, life seems to sweep you up into its flow of expectations and obligations?

I love my life. I really do.

I love my family. I love my work. I'd be hard-pressed to find ways I could be more fortunate than I am.

Still, life just seems busier than it should be. So many things feel urgent. Every small task, every opportunity feels so important.

When I can get my head above the water, when I have a

moment of solace from the fast current of expectations, I find myself wondering if my life is as it should be.

Is life just supposed to happen to me? Or is there a way to feel like I'm truly choosing the things that fill my day?

Busyness

It used to be that when I would ask a friend or acquaintance how they were doing, they would reply something like: "I'm doing good. How are you?"

Now, in response to the same question, I normally hear a slight but important addition: "Eh, I'm busy, but good. How are you?" We wear busyness like a badge of honor from a battle we wish we never fought.

Somehow busyness, in our society, connotes a degree of respect. To be busy is to be needed, to be wanted, to be valued and valuable. To be busy is to choose to be a productive member of society, a productive member of God's kingdom.

We elevate those who've built their businesses into institutions on the backs of unending hard work. We revere those people who have it all and yet seem to have limitless capacity for more.

Distraction

If there's any respite from busyness in today's society, it's usually nothing more than a form of distraction. We do much less true resting and much more avoiding. There have never been more opportunities for distraction than the day we're living in now.

In our pockets, we have a device with seemingly unlimited

potential for distraction. Social media algorithms are designed to catch and keep as much of our attention as possible. There is more sincerely entertaining television being made and presented than a reasonable person could possibly consume.

We seem, as a people, to jump from fast-paced productivity to mindless distraction, crashing into the various opportunities for escape after giving ourselves to the engine of society that never slows down and never stops.

A Different Way

But if we look at what our busyness and distraction are producing, is this way of life really working for us?

While we can marvel at the industries, the technology, the advancements achieved faster and more regularly than ever before, is the state of our humanity improving?

Is the technology we created really serving us, or are we serving it?

And are things far better in our Christian spheres? Are we unified and anointed? Are we bearing significant, visible, and eternal fruit? Do things look much better in our churches, our denominations, our institutions?

In Ephesians, Paul tells us, *"Don't waste your time on useless work, mere busywork, the barren pursuits of darkness. Expose these things for the sham they are . . . Don't live carelessly, unthinkingly. Make sure you understand what the Master wants"* (Eph. 5:11, 16–17 MSG).

If we take honest stock of the quality of the investment of our time, our money, and our talents—resources God has given us to steward—it's plain to see that we need to reset and reinvest.

We are not getting enough return on our investment. We are not healthy and thriving. Our families are not healthy and thriving. Our churches are not healthy and thriving.

And thanks be to God there is a better way. But that better way might just look a bit like an old way made new.

A Rule of Life

I first encountered the concept of a Rule of Life in reading Pete Scazerro's book, *Emotionally Healthy Spirituality*. And in a time when my life felt abundantly chaotic and scattered, his book led me through a truly transformative experience of creating intentionality for what matters most.

The Rule of Life, while not necessarily common among our modern-day expressions of faith, has a rich history in Christian tradition. The Rule of Life has roots as early as the fourth century but most notably was used by St. Benedict in the sixth century. The Rule of Life from St. Benedict facilitated a support structure for intentionality in two main ways: practices and vows (later on, we'll create our own framework).

St. Benedict encouraged the practices of "prayer, work, study, hospitality, and renewal" within the vows of "stability, conversion, and obedience."[1] If you're interested in reading more about St. Benedict's rule, there are ample free resources available online.

And in such a distracted and fragmented time, I'm noticing more and more faith communities leaning on the notions of a

Rule of Life to help them create and maintain the quality of life only intentionality can produce.

Thus, in creating a Rule for your own life, you're joining a rich history of believers both past and present, all seeking to find meaning and abundance in intentionality in God.

A Simple Definition

Simply put, a Rule of Life is a set of decisions that, when strung together, seeks to create our preferred future.

A good Rule incorporates the areas of life that matter most to us, such as spirituality and relationships, and guides us to a set of rhythms and practices so that those areas flourish.

And a good Rule is not needlessly restrictive or rigid, but something we should only really feel when it reminds us of the life we've decided we most want to live.

How to Use This Book

This resource is designed not only to help you take a step back from the day-to-day and imagine what a more intentional life could look like and produce, but I also wanted to give you a real-time opportunity to create a simple, personal, and powerful framework to facilitate the life you most want to live.

To begin, we'll explore the power of choosing to live intentionally. We'll look at a different way, a better way to view intentional decisions that looks less like rules you have to follow and more like a custom support structure birthed from desire and your uniqueness.

Then we'll explore some of the most key facets of life. Areas such as our spirituality, our relationships, our work, our time, our wirings, and our capacities to discover how we can make intentional decisions that, while simple, will have a profound impact on every part of our lives.

With each facet, we'll give you a guided time to pray, reflect, receive heavenly inspiration, and make clear decisions. With an open heart and a pen in hand, let's make space for God to reveal his better way for this life he so generously gives us every day.

Chapter 1

A Rule of Life

~

"A good rule can set us free to be our true and best selves. It is a working document, a kind of spiritual budget, not carved in stone but subject to regular review and revision. It should support us, but never constrict us."

—Margaret Guenther

I hate rules. I know there are people who would publicly say they hate rules but in secret actually love them. I am not one of those people. I *really* hate rules. And yet here I am writing a book about a Rule of Life.

What I am about to do is encourage you to not only follow a rule of sorts in guiding some of your decisions, but to build an intentional framework that will cover every important facet of your life.

In reality, rules, I think, have gotten a bad rap. And rightfully so. Most of our rules seem to have been created to prevent what we want rather than to guide us toward what we want most.

But I'm getting a bit ahead of myself.

Before we talk about building a Rule of Life, let's talk about winemaking.

Winemaking

I really like wine. I know as a Christian leader, it's not always 100 percent kosher to say I like wine. But it's the truth.

A couple of years ago while I was in Napa Valley for work (I know, my life is super hard), some friends and I were able to carve out time to visit a few wineries, and I was struck by the expansive beauty of the vineyards.

These master winemakers have built trellis after trellis, row after row, vineyard after vineyard, all to support the healthy growth of this fruit that would become wine.

They've taken the blank canvas of acres of land and created structure, purpose, and ultimately fruit. What once were empty fields after empty fields are now hundreds of expansive and flourishing vineyards. Each vineyard containing row after row filled with trellis after trellis. It's a beautiful and necessary structure in the process of creating fine wine.

Jesus loved to use nature imagery, like that found in a vineyard, to support the deep spiritual truths of the kingdom, none more beautiful than his words in John 15:5, 8 (MSG):

"I am the Vine, you are the branches. When you're joined with me and I with you, the relation intimate and organic, the harvest is

sure to be abundant. Separated, you can't produce a thing . . . This is how my Father shows who he is—when you produce grapes, when you mature as my disciples."

I love to view God as the master winemaker. He, in his grace and power, has created a system whereby we connect with him, find immeasurable life in his unceasing love and unending mercy, and bear fruit that has the power to impact eternity.

The ESV more bluntly translates these words of Jesus in John 15:5, saying, *"Apart from me you can do nothing."* But the alternative is also true! *"Whoever abides in me and I in him, he it is that bears much fruit."*

But as vineyards teach us, branches and vines actually cannot produce much fruit on their own. They need an intentional, custom support structure to share resources and bear fruit.

They need a trellis.

Trellis-building

A quick read into trellis-building, and I was hooked. I was fascinated by the beautiful connections between our inner journey and the work of trellis-building and winemaking. Where most metaphors fall short, this metaphor from Jesus seems to unfold more deeply the closer you look.

Margaret Guenther beautifully describes three facets of trellis-building that relate to our creation of a Rule of Life in her book, *At Home in the World: A Rule of Life for the Rest of Us.*[2]

First, all vines need trellises if they have a hope of bearing much fruit. Left without structure, without an intentional support system, the vines and the branches cannot create any fruit of note on their own.

Vines and branches are not strong enough to stand up on their own. And apart from intentional space created for them to grow, space created only with the addition of a trellis's support structure, they cannot bear fruit.

The same follows that without some intentionality in how you spend your time, in how you cultivate your unique wiring and calling, and in how you foster your relationships, you cannot bear the fruit of a meaningful and transformative life.

Second, not all grapes flourish in the same type of support. Different varietals need different trellis designs to help them bear the most fruit.

For example, the *vitis vinifera* varietal of grape is best suited for a low-cordon trellis to support a more vertical growth structure. Whereas Norton, Concord, and Catawba are best suited to high-cordon trellises to support their more trailing growth habits. And some hybrid-cultivars need a blend of more semi-upright support structures.[3]

God has uniquely created you. While we all need a support system of some type, the system that *I* need and that *you* need cannot be the same because *we* are not the same. That's not to say that there aren't commonalities among all good support structures. God has given each of us spiritual disciplines, stewardship principles, and similar cultural environments to bear fruit in.

But you cannot plug and play someone else's Rule of Life and expect it to be enjoyable or to support the unique growth of needed fruit that God has planned specifically for you.

And third, horticulture teaches us that you cannot tie the grapes down too tightly to the trellis and hope for them to bear much fruit. They need support but not constriction. They need structure but also freedom. Without room for mobility and spontaneity, they cannot bear much fruit.

A good Rule of Life needs to embrace the spontaneity of our God and our world while helping you identify those times that opportunities will pull you away from the life you wish rather than help create it.

In general, you should really only feel your Rule of Life when you stray too far from it. Like rumble strips on the side of the highway, you should only feel your Rule when it helps you return to the path you feel best takes you where you want to go.

And when living inside of your sense of calling and uniqueness, your trellis should barely be felt at all.

Unintentional Rules

To quote the words of Margaret Guenther again, "Consciously or unconsciously, we all follow a rule."[4] The problem is that if our Rules weren't created with intentionality, then how do we know that they will guide us into our preferred future or preferred experiences?

Or worse, how do we know that our unintentional Rule wasn't created by someone else, or perhaps even societal expectations?

How do we know that an unintentional Rule won't produce bad fruit in our lives? How do we know that these decisions won't lead us into distraction, identity crisis, or even addiction or broken relationships?

Take our use of technology and social media. Does social media truly have our best interest at heart? Or is its main goal to catch and keep as much of our attention as possible to sell that attention to advertisers, even if our attention is best placed elsewhere?

Do our employers truly have our best intention in mind? Or do they, by necessity, need to encourage and expect us to give as much of ourselves as possible to the bottom line both for our pockets and theirs?

Do restaurants and food advertisers have our best interest in mind when they present food packed with additives and sugar to lower their cost and in a way addict us further to their product?

It's no wonder that 42 percent of Americans are classified as obese, that new studies are coming out seemingly daily on the state of our social media addiction, and that workaholism has become the only socially acceptable and even encouraged form of addiction.[5]

When we look at the state of our world and the state of our own lives, we need to revisit those things that matter most to us. We need an order, a support system for those things that will actually produce life and health in ourselves and in others. We need to look at our time, our energy, our passions, our attention, and our finances and decide how we might more intentionally invest ourselves every day in order to get a better return on that investment.

We need an intentional, self-created, and God-inspired rule for our lives. We need a trellis, custom designed by us and for us, to help us live every day with a flexible intentionality that will produce the fruit of an abundant life.

Now let's talk about how we make one.

Horizontals and Verticals

A trellis in its basic definition is a grid composed of vertical posts firmly planted into the ground and horizontal lines stretching across the posts. And when I think about the building of a modern Rule of Life, something to help us create intentionality for those things that matter most, I think of two main areas of focus: facets and practices.

Facets represent major areas of our lives, such as our spirituality, our physical and emotional health, our close relationships, our work, our finances, and our media consumption.

Practices are those activities, routines, and rhythms that weave through the facets of life, such as the spiritual disciplines of prayer, of contemplation, of solitude, and of scripture reading.

Together, facets and practices serve as a system or structure of support that, when crafted with intentionality out of the genuine desire of the heart, serve to free us (rather than constrict us) to produce the fruit we so long for in our lives.

Thus, every chapter from here will include a facet of life we can explore together, as well as a guide to help you determine what intentional decisions and practices look like within that facet.

As Paul wrote in Ephesians 5:15–16, you must:

Look carefully then how you walk, not as unwise but as wise, making the best use of the time, because the days are evil.

Life is too short to let things just happen to us. There is too much opportunity for joy, for purpose, to see the beauty of heaven come to earth to simply go through the motions of life.

And in God there is a better way. We can choose how we spend our precious time and energy. We can discover that which God has called us and uniquely wired us for. And we can create an intentional guide, a trellis for our lives, that simplifies our process of living intentionally and meaningfully every day.

A Timely Guide

The rest of this resource will serve to simply be a guide for you to create a personal Rule of Life, the trellis that most serves you in your uniqueness right now.

Together, we'll explore those facets of life that are common among us, and what God and modern wisdom might say about them. I'll also provide suggested practices to help you fruitfully create and link the facets together.

Remember that this resource is for you. You alone have the ability to know how you are uniquely wired. You alone can determine the capacity and interest you have for the suggested practices.

The goal of this process is not perfection. In fact, let's just acknowledge that perfect is both impossible and unhelpful in life. It is in our weakness and failure that God seems to do his best work.

Instead, a fresh effort in a Rule of Life acknowledges that the definition of insanity is doing the same things and expecting different results. Unless we put forth a new way, an intentional way of living, we cannot hope to achieve a greater measure of abundant life or produce a greater measure of fruit.

Together, let's explore these facets and practices. May God give you the wisdom and courage to create a new way of living that is both achievable and helpful to you. And may you find peace and joy in the process.

Chapter 2

An Overarching Goal

∽

A Quick Quiz

Before we create the specifics around our facets and practices, let's talk about establishing an overarching goal. This chapter will be like picking the destination before we craft the specific route to get there.

In talking about creating an overarching goal, I'll admit I'm breaking away from the fold a bit when it comes to guides in the Rule of Life process. To be clear, I'm a goal-oriented person. I really enjoy having an overarching goal that I'm working toward, and sometimes the harder the better.

Easy feels boring to me. When something goes well, I'm ready to move on without celebrating.

My wife, who is an Enneagram seven, is the polar opposite. She lives for fun. She loves to celebrate. She lives in her strengths and focuses little on her weaknesses. That is how God has made her, and I love it. For her, the idea of an overarching goal is too restrictive and almost impossible.

So, quick quiz, do you like goals? Do you enjoy feeling like your life is adding up to one overarching objective? Or does that feel restrictive and un-fun?

If you like it, let's proceed. If you don't like goals, feel free (I mean it) to skip this chapter and head to the next one.

Freedom

When having a conversation with Christians about an overarching goal, it can be tough to free ourselves from the literal, scriptural goals God has given us for our lives. And different tribes have different versions.

Some tribes say that the goal of life is to glorify God. Some tribes say the goal of life is to love God and love people (and somehow leave out loving yourself from Jesus's words). Some tribes say your goal is to manifest faithful presence, or to advance God's kingdom in our culture. And some tribes say your life goal is evangelism and to reach the ends of the earth with the gospel.

Whew! That's a lot of main goals. And the problem with them, at least in terms of making a Rule of Life, is they just don't feel all too helpful.

Within the context of our faith, all of us are called to express a uniqueness. And that uniqueness, I believe, has elements that change and elements that stay the same from season to season.

The best overarching goals I've heard or created as it relates to a Rule of Life are both deeply personal and vigorously motivational.

The best goals should be free from shame, free from those critical inner voices we seem to carry around with us. The best goals should make us feel seen, known, and loved.

So let me say, as your de facto guide in this process, that you are free. You are free to determine what is most motivational to you. You are free to put something down and change it later. You are free to create something and show it to no one.

You are free to proof-text your overarching goal if that's helpful to you (i.e., to find a Scripture to back your intuitive emphasis). You're also free not to proof-text it.

Simply stated, you are free if you choose to be.

Finding Your Why

Developing an overarching goal for your Rule of Life is a fun but multifaceted process.

An overarching goal, even just for a season, should reflect what you know of your wiring, your calling, and your environment.

Your Wiring

So many of our questions about purpose, about our "why," relate to the age-old tension of nature versus nurture.

But in my opinion, the best way to resolve that tension is to recognize that the tension is the by-product of a false dichotomy, of splitting that which can't be split. It is not nature *versus* nurture, but nature *in relationship with* nurture.

You are who you are as a by-product of your genetics, of your family of origin, of your geography, of your relationships, and of how God has uniquely wired you.

And one of the most important elements of crafting an intentional support system for those facets of your life that matter most is understanding how you are wired.

Do you find or lose energy in the company of others? Do you primarily make decisions based on intuition, logic, or practicalities? Do you tend to think and communicate in abstract or concrete terms?

Are you primarily motivated by checking off a task list, by serving others, by achievement, by personal growth, by intellectualism, by fear, by fun, by conflict, or by harmony?

There are so many resources available for us to discover our wiring. Each of our families of origin, our subcultures, our friends, and our neighborhoods have helped shape who we are today.

Rather than seeking to be different than who you are, how can you embrace both the strengths and weaknesses of your nature and nurture and come to a sense of what matters most to you?

Give yourself the gift of valuing your likes and dislikes, your wants and don't-wants, your motivations and demotivations.

God has the power to take both that which you love and dislike about yourself and your upbringing and use it altogether in his redemptive power to guide you to a calling uniquely suited for you.

Your Calling

Paul writes in Ephesians 2:10, *"For we are his workmanship, created in Christ Jesus for good works, which God prepared beforehand, that we should walk in them."*

You have a unique calling all to your own. God has a plan for your life, a calling to make a deep and lasting impact on this earth.

In my experience, God always calls me into a position or opportunity that is a deeper and fuller expression of my wiring, of my history, and of my passions than I could have even known at the start.

Before writing First15—a daily devotional that people all around the world are using to spend meaningful time alone with God—I honestly didn't know that I liked writing. But I knew I was called. And in the process of walking out that calling in faith, I discovered that I loved the art of writing.

You have a calling that God knows is the deepest expression of who you have been and who you are becoming. He has your interest and the interest of the world around you in mind in his grace and wisdom.

Calling, like wiring, is a summation of what you know of many aspects of your life. It's a summation of the leading of the Spirit, open or closed opportunities, the wisdom of those you trust, and the capacities and expertise you've developed. Lean too heavily into one aspect of how God invites us into his will, and you might err. Ignore one aspect, and you might err as well.

But rather than putting immense pressure and weight on any one decision, in peace know that God simply asks you to be faithful with what you know today.

If you seek God, if you stay open, and if you ultimately follow what you believe to the best of your ability to be true and good, then you've done all God could ask of you, or you could ask of yourself.

More simply stated, in his seventh homily on 1 John 4:4–12, Augustine wrote:

"Love, and do what thou wilt."[6]

Know that ultimately the responsibility and opportunity is on God to guide you into his will. Simply love God and do what seems most loving and right to you.

Perfection is not the goal. The goal is simply faithfulness with what you have, who you are, and what you know.

Your Environment

In my experience, an often under-explored area of life is our environment. Too often, we take our environment, our family, our geography, our subculture, our friends and colleagues, and our industry at face value. We fail to take a step or two back from our specific part of the world to ponder at the limitations in how we were raised, in what we were taught, and the uniqueness of our value systems.

While every one of us was raised in a specific environment, we can grow and mature from that environment as opposed to simply being indoctrinated more deeply into it.

If there are values of your family of origin that are no longer serving you, you can do the inner work to thank those values and leave them behind.

If there was wounding or trauma from your upbringing, you can do the inner work to come to a healthier relationship with yourself and your world so that the wounding and trauma loses a bit of its hold on you.

If there were belief systems or expectations that you were taught from the very beginning of your life, you can still explore what beliefs and expectations are more right in your eyes.

One look at our world, and we can know two things: God is not afraid of being misunderstood, and God does not value uniformity.

Our world is full of mystery. God is a God of mystery. Truth, while real, is not always made plain. God's will, while real, is not always made plain.

No star is alike. No single creature, human or otherwise, is exactly the same. No family is the same. No church, no neighborhood, no city, no country is the same.

Somehow, all together, we both represent and misrepresent the totality of God. And that is okay. Or at least, there simply isn't another way.

Crafting intentionality in our environment by identifying areas to strengthen and to heal, by pinpointing what to hold on to and what to let go of, is a key facet of better abiding in the vine and experiencing the fruit of redemptive relationship.

Altogether

Altogether, our wirings, our callings, and our environments inform and empower us to discover our highest "why," even if that "why" changes from season to season.

While exploring each of these elements takes time and energy, the goal should be to begin now, but to begin with patience.

If we can view ourselves with the grace and patience God has for us, we can celebrate the lifelong process of discovery God invites us into.

With these three facets working together, we can hone a "why" that represents what we know of ourselves, of God, and of our world up to this point. And in doing so, acknowledge that it is in diving heart-first into the specific season we are presently in that helps us transition well into the next with grace and intentionality.

You are who you are right now, and that is good. Be nothing more. Be nothing less.

Crafting Your Goal

———————— Guided Prayer: ————————

1. Begin with stillness. Set your heart and mind, your whole being, with intention on the reality and goodness of God. Receive an awareness of his presence with you. And as you breathe, allow every exhalation to release pressure and stress, and inhalation to receive peace and courage.

2. Ask the Holy Spirit for illumination. Ask him to bring to mind aspects of your wiring, your calling, and your environment that he wants to speak to you about. Ask him for the courage to identify those places that need healing, those places to be thankful for, the most important areas of focus for your time of reflection.

3. Ask God for wisdom. As you reflect, process, and come to some loose (or initial) decisions, ask God to help you discern what is right and good in peace. Ask him to be present with you as you process. Ask him to free you from an expectation of perfection so you can run hard and fast toward joy-filled intentionality.

———————— Guided Reflection: ————————

1. How would you describe how you're wired?
What gives you energy? What motivates you? What activities, or parts of your life, do you like and dislike, and why?

_____

_____

_____

_____

2. How would you describe your sense of calling?
What opportunities has God clearly given you? What gifts has God given you? What have wise people around you said about you? What parts of the story of Scripture resonate the most with you?

_____

_____

_____

_____

3. How do you feel you're fulfilling your calling now?

How do you see your calling progressing into the future three years from now, ten years from now, twenty years from now?

_____

_____

_____

_____

4. How would you describe the environment of the family you grew up in? What stands out to you about your family of origin? What mantras did your family have? What do you see as the main values your parents raised you with, good or bad?

_____

_____

_____

_____

5. How would you describe your environment now?

What is unique about the subculture you're planted in? What do you like and dislike about those unique characteristics? What is the culture like at your work, in your family, at your church?

_____

_____

_____

_____

6. What sorts of goals do you feel rule your life right now?
How do you feel about the power those goals have?

_____

_____

_____

_____

7. What goals would you like to set for this season of your life? Write down however many come to mind. Is there a thread among them? How do they build into your preferred future? Your goal can be for a year, a few years, or more—whatever feels helpful to you!

_____

_____

_____

_____

_____

8. If you could summarize those goals, or pick the most important from among them, what would it be and why?
Remember that these are not set in stone! Give yourself freedom to grow in this process.

_____

_____

_____

_____

(Loose) Decisions:

My overarching goal for my Rule of Life is _____.

In one sentence, this overarching goal to me means _____
_____.

Suggested Practices:

Remind yourself first thing in the morning. Write down and make visible your overarching goal wherever you will see it toward the beginning of your day. A sticky note on a mirror, a phone background, a note by the coffee maker. Seek to remind yourself of what you've decided, with God, is most important for this season of your life.

Take control through journaling before starting your day. Ultimately, how you spend your time, energy, and finances is your decision. Regardless of what we say and think, this world and others in it have less of a hold on us than we might believe.

It's more about the price we're willing to pay for intentionality than the authority or control others have over us. Choose as you see your goal to take control of your life in God and invest it in the ways that seem most important to you.

Practically, a time of reflection and journaling every morning as part of your time alone with God is a powerful way to choose what to say yes and no to, and to choose what truly has power in your life.

Share your goal with those who matter most to you. The way to defend the goals we've set is through the creation of healthy boundaries. And those boundaries will impact (usually for the better over time) those who matter most to us. Decide to share your goal with your spouse, your close friends, even with your boss—not to get their buy-in but to bring them into the boundaries and intentionality you're creating for your life as a support.

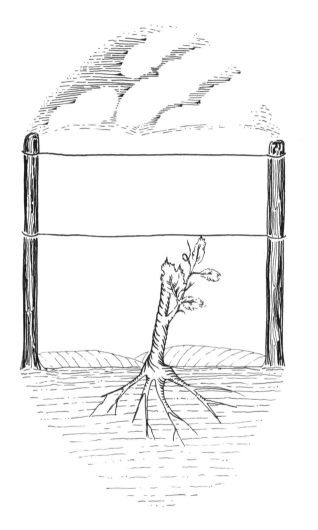

Chapter 3

Spirituality

∽

"Spirituality is recognizing and celebrating that we are all inextricably connected to each other by a power greater than all of us, and that our connection to that power and to one another is grounded in love and compassion. Practicing spirituality brings a sense of perspective, meaning, and purpose to our lives."

—Brené Brown

As we move from talking about what a Rule of Life is and isn't, and the idea of crafting an overall "why" or goal to this season, let's now take time to dive into the first and most important facet of a Rule of Life: intentional investment in our spirituality.

In Matthew 6:21, Jesus says:

"For where your treasure is, there your heart will be also."

Ultimately, where you invest yourself, your finances, your time, and your energy is where your heart will be found. And what better place to begin, what higher priority could you have, than having your heart fully found in a vibrant relationship with God?

The reality is, unless your heart is God's, no other pursuit will produce abundant life.

You could have healthy children, an amazing job, great friendships, a full bank account, but no pursuit placed higher than your pursuit of God will ultimately produce the fruit it can and should. And the opposite is also true.

Even if the circumstances of your life don't align with what the world traditionally values, if your relationship with God is thriving, it invites you into a deeper, truer sense of abundant life.

We see it in the words of Simon Peter as many of Jesus's followers were leaving in the wake of hardship, saying, *"Lord, to whom shall we go? You have the words of eternal life"* (John 6:68).

We see it in the words of Paul encouraging us to count the cost of following Jesus, saying, *"Indeed, I count everything as loss because of the surpassing worth of knowing Christ Jesus my Lord. For his sake I have suffered the loss of all things and count them as rubbish, in order that I may gain Christ"* (Philippians 3:8).

But we need look no further than the lives of the rich, the famous, those who have climbed the ladder of worldly success and found it to be unfulfilling. In God, we find abundant life given not through the ease of our circumstances, but in the midst of them. But apart from a vibrant relationship with God, all else falls short of the measure of abundant life afforded us in God's grace.

Spiritual Growth

One of the great challenges in discussing intentional investment in our spirituality comes from the notion of spiritual growth.

Try as we might, a thriving spirituality doesn't necessarily come solely through effort, although effort and discipline are elements of anything meaningful in life.

To take it further, I wonder often if even the words "spiritual growth" have done a disservice to our pursuit of God.

In the words of Jesus:

"Abide in me, and I in you. As the branch cannot bear fruit by itself, unless it abides in the vine, neither can you, unless you abide in me" (John 15:4).

A branch does not spend all its effort attempting to produce fruit. Its main objective is simply to stay connected to the vine, and fruit is the natural by-product of its connection.

You and I cannot produce the fruit of spiritual growth on our own. Growth happens, the way a grape grows from a branch, as we simply give ourselves fully to the connection with God that Jesus died to bring us.

Thus, an intentional focus on our spirituality is simply and powerfully a focus on a connection with God.

The very power of our spiritual growth lies in the fact that, in essence, it is out of our control.

But what we can control, what we can give intentionality to, is the ways in which we find and keep an abiding connection with our Father.

Creating Connection

As in all manner of things with God, when it comes to connection with him, he's already done most of the work.

At the very moment of Jesus's death, the veil signifying the separation of God's presence from his people was torn in two, top to bottom. I wonder if we spend so much effort focusing on the death of Jesus that we miss the immediate reason for his death.

God wasted no time at Jesus's death, not even a moment, tearing apart the separation sin had caused. He wasted no time allowing for the spread of his Spirit, achieving a greater closeness than we seem to have fully realized as his people.

First Corinthians 6:19 (NIV) says, *"Do you not know that your bodies are temples of the Holy Spirit, who is in you, whom you have received from God?"*

The very Spirit of God is right now fellowshipping with your spirit (1 John 4:13).

Creating connection with God is far more about subtraction than addition. The connection between you and God already exists. The work of spiritual connection is more about the removal of distraction, the freedom from shame, the seeing of truth, the consistent focus needed to remember, to experience, and to learn to live with an abiding connection with the God who never leaves us.

A Rule for Our Spirituality

As we think about how, with intention, to create a Rule of Life for our spirituality, luckily, we have centuries of practice and wisdom from those who have gone before us.

Rhythm for Connection

Perhaps the most important element of a Rule of Life for our spirituality is creating a rhythm for connecting with God that we can stick to.

There are loads of historic practices to pull from. Take, for example, the concept of The Daily Office, crafted readings and prayers for morning, noon, and night.

Or take The Examen, a practice introduced by St. Ignatius, of ending our days in reflection on the hours past, inviting God to heal and speak his wisdom into our days before the next one begins.

Or in the evangelical tradition, there's commonly a value for beginning the day alone with God, incorporating some of the basic elements of engaging with God, such as Scripture reading, prayer, journaling, and worship.

Most important to remember is that a rhythm for connecting with God is an invitation, not an obligation. We need feel no shame when we miss one of our rhythms with God, because shame only serves to drive us further apart.

God is ecstatic, I think, to have any and every moment we would give to him, no matter how many moments we've spent living as if we were without him.

Without a regular rhythm of focusing all of our attention on God, where we remember, experience, and take hold of this connection between his Spirit and ours, it is simply too easy to spend our days distracted and busy with things that cannot bear fruit.

Like a trellis, we need a structure we can loosely attach ourselves to in our pursuit of God.

I begin every day in reading, in silence, in honest reflection, and in prayer. When I can, I take time at noon and in my final moments awake to invite God, even for a few minutes, to reveal his presence afresh.

I take a day a week, a Sabbath, to set aside busyness and enjoy God as fully as I can in time alone with him, with my family, with my hobbies, and with my community.

I also take around a week a year to do some form of a spiritual retreat, to get extended and free time to engage my heart with God without distraction or a need to watch the clock. But remember, the goal is to create a trellis that suits *you*.

As good winemakers build a custom trellis for the uniqueness of the vine, there is freedom for you to build the rhythm that is most helpful and achievable for you.

You should find that your rule for your spirituality is only something you feel when you're straying too far from your intention with God.

Life-giving Practices

Beyond the rhythm you create, it's vital to find the elements or practices that can most help you connect with God.

Remember, this is not an obligation. This is not a box to check. This isn't like lifting weights where you progress through a system to experience physical growth.

This is a relationship.

And like any relationship, things can change from season to season. Things that used to excite you can begin to feel rote. Things that used to feel rote might now fill your soul. The goal is vibrancy in your relationship, not a perfect practice.

Within that goal, it's incredibly important to make a flexible plan for your time of connection with God. We are simply too busy and too distracted to give our attention to something we're not sure is going to be fruitful.

Making a plan for those practices that you feel will be most beneficial in experiencing and keeping an abiding connection with God is vital.

My plan is beginning with a journal to start my time with God and myself in an honest and transparent manner. From there, I move to about ten minutes of silence, focusing my attention simply on my awareness of self and of God. Then I worship, I read, and I pray.

All in all, my rhythm can shrink to as few as fifteen minutes or extend as long as an hour in the morning. I allow my hunger, God's leadership, and my morning responsibilities to determine what my time with God looks like.

At lunch, if I can, I love to take five or ten minutes to simply sit in solitude. Our days can be so stimulating, it's amazing what ten minutes of quiet reflection can do for our minds and our hearts.

In the evening, if possible, I love to practice the Examen, where I review my day with God and allow him to speak his words of wisdom and healing before I move into sleep and then another day.

On my Sabbath, I try when possible to get extended time with God in reading and in longer times of meditation and prayer.

On a spiritual retreat, I try to follow the guidance of a spiritual director, or a plan I create for myself if I have a spiritual area of study I'm interested in.

But these are the rhythms *I've* chosen. To be frank, a large part of my vocational responsibilities hinge on the depth of my connection with God. I am called and wired for deep investment of my whole being into the pursuit of unfiltered and unfettered connection with God.

Only you can know what you are called to, what you are wired for, and what is achievable for you.

So my encouragement for you as you craft your rule is to begin not with too much, but with a simple and achievable goal for your spirituality. Don't set yourself up for failure from the start.

How much better to watch your rule for your spirituality grow over time with you than to be an admirable but unachievable goal that's simply impossible for you, at least in this season.

Crafting Your Spiritual Rule

──────────────── Guided Prayer: ────────────────

1. Take a moment to focus your heart and mind on the availability of God's presence. Don't craft an intention behind your spirituality as if you aren't connected with God already. Allow a present sense of his presence to fuel your time of reflection.

2. Ask the Spirit to make clear God's invitation to meet with you in this season. Pay attention to any sense you get from the Spirit around why God longs to meet with you, or even what a rule for your spirituality could look like.

3. Surrender your whole being to the pursuit of God. Commit to make space for whatever your relationship with God needs to thrive. Acknowledge that God's highest commandment, and therefore his best plan for your life, is to simply love him with your whole being.

──────────────── Guided Reflection: ────────────────

1. Write down what your rhythm for connecting with God looks like now.

How often are you spending time in prayer, reading, and worship? In what ways is your connection corporate and private?

_____

_____

_____

_____

2. Why do you want to create intentionality around your rhythm for connecting with God?
What has your life looked like in times when your relationship with God was vibrant? What does your life look like when it's not? Why does your spirituality matter to you?

_____

_____

_____

_____

_____

3. What elements of spirituality are meaningful for you right now? What do you find helps you connect with God the most? What possible normative spiritual disciplines aren't helpful to you right now?

_____

_____

_____

_____

_____

4. If you had fifteen minutes to connect with God, how would you want to spend them?

If it's helpful, think about three five-minute practices.

_____

_____

_____

_____

5. If you had an hour to connect with God, how would you want to spend it?

If it's helpful, think about four fifteen-minute practices.

_____

_____

_____

_____

6. What aspects of spirituality are you most interested in discovering more about?

Where could you see yourself investing your time in learning as an aspect of your rule for spirituality?

_____

_____

_____

_____

7. What rhythms beyond a daily one would you like to engage in for your spirituality? Maybe it's a midday or evening practice. Maybe it's a form of a retreat. What else would be worth your investment of time and energy?

_____

_____

_____

_____

8. Which thoughts that you've written down so far bring you peace, and which bring you pressure?
Remember, this is an invitation, not an obligation. The elements of a rule for spirituality you will actually practice must have at least a sense of authentic desire to them.

_____

_____

_____

_____

(Loose) Decisions:

My plan for consistent (or daily) investment in my spirituality is _____.

The spiritual practices for connection that I'm most interested in are _____.

I want to discover more about my spirituality in the areas of _____.

In one sentence, an intentional investment in my spirituality to me looks like _____.

Suggested Practices:

Worship. I find that engaging in some form of worship—whether through song or declaration or simply affection in my heart turned toward God—places God at the center of my spirituality instead of me. What I need most desperately is his grace and his goodness at the center of my time with him so it can, in turn, be at the center of my life.

Read. Engaging our minds and our hearts with a rule for our spirituality is a critical component of a thriving relationship with God. I believe that incorporating both Scripture and other resources is a beautiful, meaningful pairing to my daily time with God, as well as other moments in my day.

Pray. Perhaps the most important element in a rule for our spirituality is true conversation with God. I find that when I've genuinely spoken with God and listened to him, my spirituality thrives. When I simply fill my mind or talk at him, my spirituality begins to feel stale and stagnant. Spirituality is a relationship. And all relationships need consistent and vulnerable conversation.

Chapter 4

Health

∽

"If a man is to live, he must be all alive, body, soul, mind, heart, spirit."

—Thomas Merton

The more complicated my life and our world gets, the more I realize that good health doesn't just happen.

But before you think this is a chapter on eating salads, let's take a step back for a moment.

Biblical Health

One of the sentiments of Scripture that we have a tendency to interpret incorrectly relates to the different aspects of our being. At times, we break apart the scriptural references to our being into the categories of soul, spirit, and body, which is referred to as tripartite theology.

In turn, we think about health, priorities, and even ways that we love and serve God into categories that biblically aren't meant to be separated.

In declaring the most important commandment, Jesus says in Luke 10:27, *"You shall love the Lord your God with all your heart and with all your soul and with all your strength and with all your mind."*

But Jesus isn't intending to encourage separation of the parts of us, or even a strategy to categorize the aspects of the way we love God.

Instead, he was deploying a common rabbinic teaching principle of hyperbole from the time to emphasize the need for us to simply love God with our whole being. He's saying that because we know the heart, soul, mind, and strength can't be separated in this life, we're to engage in a holistic process of loving God.

It isn't enough for us to tithe. It isn't enough for us to work hard. It isn't enough for us to contemplate or study or teach. God's highest commandment is to love him with all we are and all we have.

You see the same rabbinic teaching principle at play in Hebrews 4:12, which says, *"For the word of God is living and active, sharper than any two-edged sword, piercing to the division of soul and of spirit, of joints and of marrow, and discerning the thoughts and intentions of the heart."*

The author of Hebrews isn't intending to say that soul and spirit can be separated, or joints and marrow. He's simply saying that Scripture is so sharp it could separate that which can never be separated. It's a form of exaggeration to demonstrate the power of God's word.

Holistic Health

Biblical health is holistic health, because God cares about the whole of us as a person. For instance, the book of Proverbs is laden with exhortations to cultivate health in uncommon ways.

Proverbs 14:30 says, *"A tranquil heart gives life to the flesh, but envy makes the bones rot."*

Proverbs 3:7–8 says, *"Be not wise in your own eyes; fear the LORD, and turn away from evil. It will be healing to your flesh and refreshment to your bones."*

Proverbs 17:22 says, *"A joyful heart is good medicine, but a crushed spirit dries up the bones."*

In Philippians 4, we discover an encouragement that through prayer, supplication, and thanksgiving, we can find a peace offered to us not through our circumstances, but in the midst of them.

And speaking to the value of physical health, 1 Corinthians 6:19–20 says, *"Or do you not know that your body is a temple of the Holy Spirit within you, whom you have from God? You are not your own, for you were bought with a price. So glorify God in your body."*

For the purposes of this guide to intentional living, we'll look at physical, emotional, and mental health both interdependently and independently. And in developing a Rule of Life for our holistic health, we'll find how our health deeply affects our quality of life, either for the better or worse.

Physical Health

Out of these three facets of holistic health, I feel the least equipped to exhort you to physical health. I love to eat, and I don't particularly enjoy many of the commonly encouraged fitness activities.

At times in my adult life, I've been fairly physically healthy, and at other times, I've bordered on obesity. I can say that just recently in the past year of writing this book, I have been sincerely convicted and felt a genuine pull toward greater physical health.

Maybe it's a desire to keep up with my two growing boys and their energy. Maybe it's a desire to feel more comfortable in social situations with my appearance. Maybe it's a desire to sleep better. Honestly, it's probably a combination of a lot of factors.

What I do know is that I don't really like a lot of the encouragement out there toward physical health.

It seems to me that we have a really unhealthy relationship with our physical appearance. Society puts before us unachievable standards of appearance as the standard of beauty. In our world, beauty is not inherent in all that God has made, but a judgment made based on comparison to that which is often fabricated and manufactured.

But at the same time, I think Scripture and our human experience tell us that physical health *does* matter. Our physical health affects our quality of life. The way we eat and engage in physical activity affects our relationships, our energy levels, our sense of self, and even our ability to think, feel, and act with clarity and purpose.

Activity

Related to physical activity, I love this thought from John F. Kennedy:

> Physical fitness is not only one of the most important keys to a healthy body, it is the basis of dynamic and creative intellectual activity.

Being physically active truly does have a remarkable effect on the rest of our being.

As a bonus, physical activity is proven to have a real impact on our risk for depression, our anxiety levels, and our ability to sleep well.[8]

Exercise is proven to lower our risk of cardiovascular disease, type 2 diabetes, and even some cancers.[9]

The CDC says simply, "People who are physically active for about 150 minutes a week have a 33% lower risk of all-cause mortality than those who are physically inactive."[10]

If we are to glorify God in our bodies and achieve the level of abundant life I believe we're after, then our physical activity is a critical component of a meaningful Rule of Life.

Nutrition

But physical activity alone isn't enough to produce a higher quality of life and health.

First Corinthians 10:31 says, *"So, whether you eat or drink, or whatever you do, do all to the glory of God."*

I love the sentiment from this anonymous quote:

What you eat literally becomes you. You have a choice in what you're made of.

I believe that our food consumption has gone much the way of the rest of our society.

We eat what is easy, whether or not what is easy is good. Like our media consumption, much of the food manufactured for us is intended to be addictive. The goal of these companies is not our health, but more of our money.

Foods manufactured with high amounts of processed fats and sugars are addictive to our bodies while giving us little to no nutritional value.

Forty-two percent of the American population is categorized as obese as of 2020, up 26 percent from 2008.[11]

Obesity affects our children, costs our nation over $150 billion dollars in medical care and other costs, is worse in groups of lower socioeconomic status, and isn't getting better.[12]

But the solution isn't to deprive ourselves of good food either. As a facet of a Rule of Life, there's an opportunity to reclaim the beauty of good food. There's an opportunity to celebrate the abundance of nutrition God has given us in his creation.

How astounding is it that what we need to survive and thrive has been given to us in God's creation? And that in

God's creativity, there are wonderful ways to prepare this food so that it's both healthy and deeply satisfying. But to enjoy the opportunity before us related to nutrition, we need to swim upstream from our culture.

Whereas our culture is heading toward greater speed, greater levels of addiction, and higher degrees of obesity, we need to choose to slow down, to learn again how to prepare food, and to actually enjoy what God has given us rather than fill our stomachs with what is quick, easy, and cheap on our way from activity to activity.

Sleep

Beyond our physical activity and nutrition, we need good sleep.

The past few years or so, I've struggled with a form of insomnia. I'm often awake in the earliest parts of the morning, my mind racing and impeding my ability to fall back asleep. Across the past few years while seeing the difference a lack of sleep makes on the rest of my life, I've become incredibly intentional with sleep.

Somewhere around 35 percent of Americans are sleep-deprived, as defined as less than seven hours a night by the CDC. Sleep is directly tied to other factors of health, such as depression, coronary heart disease, and heart attacks.[13]

Today, there are a lot of factors at odds with getting a healthy amount of sleep. With the ability for most of us to work anywhere and anytime, it can be really difficult to ward off the pressure to work later at night or earlier in the morning.

With all the stimulation from electronic devices, and the norm of consuming media of some form all the way up to our time to sleep, our brains can have an immensely challenging time falling into a deep sleep and a normal sleep rhythm.

Plus, with all the challenges at odds with our physical activity, nutrition, and sleep, we need to recognize that achieving a good measure of holistic health will look like swimming upstream in today's culture.

Swim Upstream

For our sake and the sake of those we love, we need to fulfill the command of 1 Corinthians 6:20: *"So glorify God in your body."*

God has given us what we need in our bodies and in our earth to enjoy creating and sustaining physical health.

Regardless of where you are with your physical health journey right now, your body is highly skilled at healing itself. It's never too late to work toward and find physical health.

The decisions you make each day with your activity, nutrition, and sleep will bring a real measure of abundant life when you add them together—and quicker than you might think.

Be patient. Be proactive. Swim upstream from your culture. And in developing a rule for your physical health, discover how it can create a more solid foundation for every other facet of your life.

Emotional Health

Somehow, at least within the evangelical expression of Christianity, emotions have gotten a bad rap.

In our pursuit of truth, we have come to a degree of distrust and passivity in regard to our emotions and the emotions of others.

I believe there is such a thing as objective truth. But to disregard our emotions in the pursuit of truth is, in fact, to limit all the tools God has given us in the discovery of truth.

Whether our emotions are true or not, they are real, they are valid, and they are at least an important gateway to our discovery of truth. What our bodies tell us about our stress, what they tell us about our relationships, what they tell us about our experience of God and his world are vital pieces of the puzzle in the fullness of our experience of life.

The pathway to a healthy relationship with our emotions, and to allowing God to use them fully for his glory and our good, does not include a denial or disregard for them.

Rather, we need to understand that our emotions have a lot to tell us, especially if we're emotionally healthy.

When healthy, our emotions can help us discern a deeper truth than might be perceived simply through logic or reason. An abundant life should be soaked in abundant emotions, not void of them.

Often, truth and abundant life are based in subtleties felt before considered, intuited as a beginning of the journey to full understanding.

To craft an intentionality to our life is to create space for increasing awareness, validation, and discovery of what we're feeling, why we're feeling it, and what God might say about our feelings.

Mental Health

It's often the unseen parts of one's health, or unhealth, that have the most dramatic effects on quality of life. While challenging, there's something that's easier to validate and treat when your health issues are physical.

If you damage a part of your body, there's a doctor and process for treatment and recovery with the goal of returning to normal life. For your weight, there are ample ways to diet and exercise to get into a healthier physical state.

But your mental health lies under the surface.

I often feel like my mind should just be fine without much care or intentionality. When I'm struggling with my mental health, it can be incredibly difficult to validate even legitimate reasons why I'm hurting. When I'm doing well, it can feel like that should just be normal as opposed to something to learn from or even celebrate.

In my disregard for my mental health, I can suffer from perspectives about myself, my world, and my closest relationships that deserve the same level of respect, of focus, and of treatment that my physical body does.

Everything we think, everything we feel, everything we choose to do occurs through the filter of our mind. For better or worse, we cannot see ourselves or others apart from our mental narratives and perspectives.

So, in turn, the way we view the entirety of our life will be filtered through the state of our mental well-being.

Honest Assessment

Altogether, our physical, mental, and emotional health has a profound impact on our quality of life and our ability to engage in meaningful action.

When one facet of our health suffers, we suffer. When we are mentally, emotionally, and physically healthy, it's like our true selves are unlocked and we're able to finally exhibit the fullest expression of our unique wiring and calling to our benefit and the benefit of every person around us.

What if Christians were known for being the healthiest of humans? What if we were known for our emotional and mental fortitude? What if we were physically healthy, not out of the value of comparison, but out of a goal of a truly abundant life?

Imagine the story our lives would tell if we sought to simply be as healthy as possible.

As you craft a rule for your health, take an honest assessment of where you are without being too harsh with yourself. Adopt the view of grace that your heavenly Father has for you. Recognize how hard it can be to achieve health in the society we're living in.

But acknowledge that God has given you the strength, the resources, and the fortitude to fight for your health every day.

Think about what your life could be if it were built on the solid foundation of holistic health. Create a rule that helps you put intentionality behind the great opportunity before you.

Crafting a Rule for Health

——————————— Guided Prayer: ———————————

1. Ask God for a sense of his grace over your health. Seek to begin your time of prayer, reflection, and rule creation with honest grace.

2. Ask God why health matters from his perspective. Think about how God created our bodies for health. Think about the ways he created physical activity, nutrition, rest, emotions, and our minds. And seek to see it all as good.

3. Ask God to guide you to an achievable and motivational rule for your health. Notice a sense of God's Spirit fellowshipping with your spirit before you begin.

——————————— Guided Reflection: ———————————

1. What has health meant to you? What has physical, emotional, and mental health looked like for you in the past? Become aware of a sense of your current definition of health, whether created intentionally or unintentionally.

_____

_____

_____

_____

2. What aspects of health do you value already?
Where are you already doing well as it relates to your health?

_____

_____

_____

**3. What aspects of health need the most intention from
you in this season?** To get a greater sense of holistic health,
where do you need to create more space or invest more
intentionality with your time, energy, or learning?

_____

_____

_____

_____

4. What could a rule for your physical health look like?
What sorts of activities would be meaningful and achievable
for you in this physical season?

_____

_____

_____

_____

5. What could a rule for your emotional health look like?
How can you get a better sense of your emotional health, and
what sorts of practices could help you foster a greater degree
of emotional health?

_____

_____

_____

_____

6. What could a rule for your mental health look like?

What affects you most mentally? When do you feel healthiest mentally? What sort of intention could you put behind the goal of being mentally healthy?

_____

_____

_____

_____

_____

7. Are there any commonalities among practices or rhythms for your holistic health? Is there one practice or rhythm that seems to have a positive effect on one or more areas of your health? Are there factors that negatively affect one or more areas of your health?

_____

_____

_____

_____

8. What would be three key health practices that could increase your level of holistic health in this season?

Instead of overhauling every facet of your health, what are three practices, rhythms, or disciplines that are achievable and would have a real and positive impact on your quality of life?

(Loose) Decisions:

I plan on investing in my physical health in this next season by _____.

I plan on investing in my emotional health in this next season by _____.

I plan on investing in my mental health in this next season by _____.

To make space for an investment in my health, I need to _____.

Suggested Practices:

Eat a healthy breakfast. Beginning our day with a glass of water and a quick and healthy breakfast sets us on a path of intentional investment in our well-being. I find it so much easier to eat healthy throughout the day when I'm building on an earlier, healthy choice.

Turn off your screens forty-five minutes before you intend to fall asleep. In order to reach a deep sleep, our brains need space from the stimulation of screens, both because of their light and because of the content of our media. Setting an alarm to turn off your screens forty-five minutes before you intend to go to sleep helps you *fall* asleep and *stay* asleep longer. It also helps you create some consistency to your sleep schedule.

Consider therapy. Whether I feel I'm doing well or not mentally and emotionally, I find going to therapy every week has a profoundly positive impact on almost every area of my life. It helps me engage with greater awareness and empathy in my relationships. It helps me process my interior life. It helps me find healing and perspective. Through one hour a week of therapy, you truly can find a significant lift in your overall well-being.

Chapter 5

Relationships

〜

"To love is to be vulnerable."
—C. S. Lewis

Somehow, as a society, we've ventured away from that which really produces a meaningful life: relationships. Simply take a look at the lives of those who have status and money but lack meaningful relationships.

What are beautiful possessions if you have no one to share them with? How often do we see celebrity become a burden to the quality of life of our most famous?

Mass appeal is in no way a substitute for meaningful relationships. In fact, it's often a hindrance.

In the age of online relationships, where we see only what others want us to see, where our communication feeds are more of a vacuum of agreement or incendiary thinking than honest dialogue and true connection, to what degree do these online friendships really produce a higher quality of life?

In fact, a study conducted by the American Journal of Preventative Medicine concluded that social media is both our greatest opportunity for social connection and our greatest source of loneliness.[14]

We have a problem when it comes to intentionality in our relationships. Our world no longer seems to support or encourage the development and ongoing investment of those relationships in which we alone can find abundant life. When relational equity is measured in likes, reposts, followers, and digital friends, it's clear we need to look for a different way of cultivating relationships.

As it is with much of our life, we have an opportunity to chart a new path. We have an opportunity to craft an intentionality to relationship that, in turn, sets aside that which is fake, that which is comparison-driven, that which has no hope of benefiting us or our world in pursuit of a greater opportunity.

God

Having given a whole facet to our spirituality, I'll save time here in terms of our relationship to God.

But in the context of this whole facet on relationship, I do want to note that God himself models a perfect relationship for us in his relationship with himself.

A paradox to our faith is the existence of a perfect, triune God. That God in himself is both three and one. The Father, the Son, and the Spirit in perfect unity make up God as we know him. Each humbled and in service before the other. Each fully God. Each fully connected with the others.

There is no framework for us living a life alone, as we are made in the image of this divine, loving relationship. And in this image, we reflect and imitate not just a single facet of his nature, but we reflect and imitate the complete and triune God.

As we seek to develop an intentionality to meaningful relationships, there is no more vital relationship to cultivate than that of the triune God. A relationship with him is the foundation and source of empowerment for every other meaningful relationship we develop.

Marriage

Apart from God, there is no greater source of encouragement or discouragement in our quality of life than our marriage.

When healthy, marriage provides a support system and a depth of connection unmatched by any other relationship.

There's a reason God most often equates our relationship with him to that of a bride and bridegroom.

Marriage is constant sacrifice. It is a greater measure of life found through losing than seeking to keep. It is a depth of knowledge that goes beyond words. It is heart-given and woven into one's heart. It is affirmation and affection in the good and the bad circumstances, and at our personal best and worst.

Marriage is a relationship that deepens through suffering, grows closer through hardship, strengthens through embodying vulnerability, and provides courage the more our weaknesses are made visible.

But when a marriage is suffering, there is no facet of life that depth of suffering doesn't affect. In marital struggle, our joy suffers, our calling suffers, and our sense of self suffers. In marriage, we are given to another in true connection and covenant. This other person becomes like a part of ourselves.

To fight, divide, and bicker is like warring within ourselves.

Too often, I see marriages suffer under the guise of a sense of calling to ministry to others, as if (for those who are married) marriage isn't far more primary than any other calling in our lives.

Our marriages deserve whatever they require to flourish.

And if, as Scripture has told us, our marriages are meant to be a pure and visible reflection of Christ's love for his people, what better investment in intentionality can we make for the sake of the gospel than cultivating vibrant and healthy marriages?

When looking at the state of marriage within the church, we have significant work before us. Just because we're believers, and just because we engage in Christian community, does not mean our marriages will flourish.

These vital relationships will not stay healthy on their own. They need cultivation. They need investment. They need our attention, our emotional investment, our time, and our loving care.

It's exhilarating to think what we can achieve through a vibrant and thriving marriage. There could be no greater gift for the earth than the example of a loving, sacrificial, and life-giving marriage.

A Note on Divorce

In speaking about marriage, I in no way want to shame or devalue those reading this who have gone through a divorce. I cannot know your story. I cannot know your struggles.

If you have gone through a divorce, I understand how limited the grace and empathy is within the church for your experience.

There is grace upon grace for us all in the good and the hard, whether our experience is singleness, marriage, divorce, or a form of relational combination.

A Note on Singleness

If you have yet to be married, or you're on the other side of a marriage, whether by loss or divorce, you can absolutely craft an intentionality to your singleness.

Feel free to use this section for dating, engagement, preparation for dating, or simply as a note to consider for the future for wherever life may take you relationally.

Children

As of writing this, I have two boys, Wesley and Wells, who are four and two. When I had kids, it felt like my life went from a fairly calm ocean to a turbulent sea.

Before kids, there were waves with both highs and lows, but the highs and lows were less chaotic and they seemed to come and go less frequently.

In having kids, the waves have a greater height and a lower low and come far more often.

I remember when Wesley was little, I would go from audibly saying as I held him asleep in my arms that "life cannot possibly get better," to declaring that I could kill him since I could not get his screaming under control—all within the span of thirty minutes.

Now, before you call child services on me, I didn't actually mean I could kill him. Are there any parents who haven't said they could kill their kids? I haven't met any. If you know any, send their information my way so I can glean some peace and wisdom from them.

All that to say, kids are both incredibly beautiful and incredibly challenging. My boys need and want more than I could ever have to give. But somehow, loving them every day increases my capacity to love.

Somehow, a part of my soul opens around them that seems to know no bounds.

There isn't one thing I wouldn't do for them if they truly needed me. And there isn't a day that could go by when I wouldn't be able to genuinely love them in the most core part of me.

But I would be a fool to think that my relationship with my children would thrive without intentionality. I am too busy. And even at four and two, my children are too busy.

I have seen too many families who, on the basis of busyness, seem to miss out on the cultivation of true purpose, true relationship, and true love in the context of their children.

In a world that simply asks too much of us as parents, and

too much of our children, we need to develop an intentionality to our relationship with our children if we are to experience the true quality of life that comes from a vibrant and connected family unit.

Community

Finally, on the basis of a depth of life in our relationship with God, with our spouse, and with our children, we have the capacity and empowerment needed to engage in a loving relationship with this world we find ourselves in.

I honestly believe we get our priorities almost backward when it comes to our communities.

The need of our world is so great, the call from God to impact our world so real, that too often we sacrifice our relationship with our children, with our spouse, and with God out of service to this world.

But truly, what do we have to offer this world if our nearest relationships aren't thriving? Does the world really need more empty messages of hope, where our words are true but our lives fail to exhibit the fruit of truth?

On the basis of thriving relationships in those areas that matter most, we'll find a true capacity to serve and love in a way where our words and our lives declare the goodness and reality of God.

On the basis of thriving relationships, we'll be able to show up to work fulfilled and humble, not requiring our performance or workplace status to define us and give us a sense of identity and purpose.

On the basis of thriving relationships, we'll be able to show up to church full and ready to have something to give in unity and humility rather than asking the church to serve our needs for spiritual and relational connection and purpose.

On the basis of thriving relationships, we'll be able to share God's message of hope and restored relationship with a world that thinks they have to vie and fight for limited access to a selfish love. The light of God's unconditional love and grace will shine through us, inviting even the most disillusioned among us to see a deeper and better way to live on the basis of God's unceasing and grace-filled love.

Setting aside Perfection

Before this sounds like way too much to engage with intentionally, it's important to remember that the simple, positive, actionable steps you can take now toward cultivating meaningful and vibrant steps will lead you to where you want to go.

In the context of relationships, perfection is absolutely impossible. There is no perfect relationship with God. There is no perfect marriage. There is no perfect family. There is no perfect community.

But there is an invitation from God to engage every day in his new mercies, to seek to love and be loved by him and others as deeply and as purely as possible.

As you craft a rule for your relationships, seek to simply implement that which is achievable *now*. There are seasons to relationships. There are stages to relationship development.

Recognize where you are right now and recognize what you have capacity and knowledge for. Know that positive action and engagement now will absolutely lead you to greater opportunities for loving relationships in the future.

Crafting a Rule for Relationships

———————————— Guided Prayer: ————————————

1. Ask God for inspiration of purpose when it comes to your relationships. Commit to allowing the Spirit to redefine what your life is about and to reframe how you invest yourself in what truly matters.

2. Reflect for a moment on the very nature of God as a relationship. Think about God as three in one: Father, Son, and Spirit. Reflect on what that reality might mean for you as a being made in the image of a relationship.

3. Surrender your notions of worldly success to pick up God's notions of a meaningful life through meaningful relationships. Commit to changing the way you spend your time and your energy, even if it means losing worldly success.

Guided Reflection:

1. In what ways do meaningful relationships matter to you already? How are you already giving your time and energy to the cultivation of meaningful relationships? Which relationships matter most to you right now?

_____

_____

_____

_____

2. In what ways are you excelling in your relationships? Where would you say you've cultivated meaningful relationships? Who do you genuinely know well, and who are you known well by?

_____

_____

_____

_____

3. In what ways do you struggle with intentionality in your relationships? Do you struggle to let yourself be known? Do you struggle to listen well or to make space in the rest of your busyness for relationships?

_____

_____

_____

_____

_____

_____

4. What most keeps you from fostering meaningful relationships? Whether emotional or practical, what are those barriers that you would like to eliminate so you can sincerely thrive in your relationships?

_____

_____

_____

_____

5. List the relationships you feel most called to foster (apart from your relationship with God). Who has God called you to long term, or simply for this season? Who do you want most to be close with?

_____

_____

_____

_____

6. What sorts of practices or investments of time, energy, or vulnerability will help foster those relationships?
Think about them individually. What could you do that would help these relationships grow? What do these individuals find most loving? What do you find loving and fun?

_____

_____

_____

_____

7. What do you need to let go of or change to create the space needed to foster those relationships? Think about them individually. What barriers can you remove to go deeper?

_____

_____

_____

_____

8. What could your life look like if those relationships were all thriving? Imagine your life with these key relationships sincerely thriving. What would that do for your quality of life? How would that empower your ability to live out your calling?

_____

_____

_____

_____

(Loose) Decisions:

I plan on intentionally investing in these relationships across the next season: _____.

Rhythms or practices that will most help me create thriving relationships would be _____.

To make space for an intentional investment in my relationships, I will _____.

Suggested Practices:

Cultivate vulnerability. Even in our closest relationships, it can be hard to be vulnerable. But time spent with others by itself doesn't promise depth in those relationships. It's vulnerability that cultivates real trust and meaning. Seek to cultivate true vulnerability with others. Tell them what they mean to you—often. Share your frustrations. Be the one who is clear and kind. And open the door with your intentionality for them to do the same.

Learn love languages. Our time and money will go much further in cultivating meaningful relationships if we invest ourselves in ways others find most loving. Normally, we love others the way we prefer to be loved. But loving others in the way they prefer to receive love makes a far more significant impact on our depth in relationships.

Repurpose existing rhythms. Instead of watching television or working over a meal, use that time to cultivate real relationships at home and at work. Instead of listening to the radio in the car, give a friend a quick call just to see how they're doing. Instead of scrolling through social media, ask your friends honest questions or tell them what they mean to you. Meaningful relationships don't necessarily require more hours—just more intentionality.

Relationships

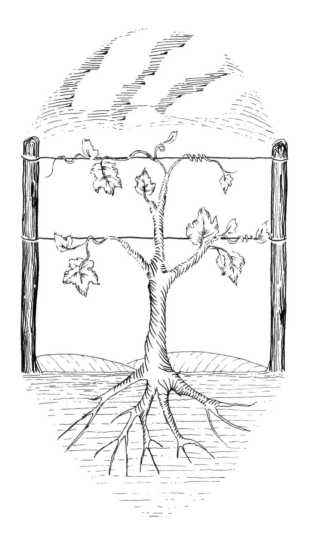

Chapter 6

Media Consumption

～

"Distracted from distraction by distraction."
—T. S. Eliot

Any modern Rule of Life, I believe, has to contain intentionality related to our media consumption.

Media throughout the ages has always had a pull on our attention, and I'm not one who would say that's always a bad thing. Experiences normally categorized as entertainment can be refreshing and moving. Entertainment can help build empathy, knowledge, and connection and can even have a profoundly positive impact on our lives.

But the media we're experiencing today given its increasing availability, the number of screens we're surrounded by, and the increasingly addictive nature of social media needs a massive

Living Intentionally

amount of intentionality, self-awareness, and self-discipline if we are to be healthy and whole humans while we consume it.

Before I sound too apocalyptic about the state of our media (if I haven't yet, I might in a minute), I do want to acknowledge that with every development of new media, our societal experts sort of have a period of freaking out.

A Brief History of Media Criticism

Upon the birth of printed materials, Socrates famously warned against them because they would "create forgetfulness in the learners' souls, because they will not use their memories."

In describing the development of curriculum and the education system, an 1883 article in the medical journal the *Sanitarian* said that schools would "exhaust the children's brains and nervous systems with complex and multiple studies, and ruin their bodies by protracted imprisonment."[15] And twelve-year-old Craig agrees.

In 1936, a music magazine called the *Gramophone* criticized the radio, saying that children had "developed the habit of dividing attention between the humdrum preparation of their school assignments and the compelling excitement of the loudspeaker."[16]

In 1949, in reference to the television, the famed theologian Reinhold Niebuhr, author of the Serenity Prayer, predicted that "much of what is still wholesome in our lives will perish under the impact of this visual aid."[17]

Some of these criticisms sound incredibly accurate, some sound outlandish, and some sound as if they will simply need more time to determine if they hold true.

88

While we may not know the long-term effects of our modern state of media, we can come to a deeper awareness around the current, personal effects of media on our quality of life.

We can craft an intentionality toward our experience of media while the experts unfold its more holistic effects on us as a society.

A Criticism of Modern Media

As of writing this guide to a modern Rule of Life, there's a lot surfacing into the broader minds of our society around the detrimental effects of modern media.

The documentary *The Social Dilemma* profoundly unearths the principle that with social media, we are not the customer, but the product. The financial goals of social media companies are driven by their ability to catch and keep our attention so they can sell our attention to advertisers.

Through the development of highly effective algorithms, these companies are addicting us to their platforms, because greater attention caught and kept equals greater profits.

Thus, our social media addiction is having a profoundly negative impact on our well-being.

In the *American Journal of Epidemiology*, a study found that regular usage of Facebook had a "negative impact on an individual's well-being." [18]

In Schwab's 2019 *Modern Wealth* survey, they found that 49 percent of millennials said that social media played an important role in overspending their finances. [19]

In 2013, a Journal of Consumer Research study linked heavy

social media use with credit card debt and a higher body mass index.[20]

In a 2018 study from the Journal of Social and Clinical Psychology, those who limited their social media to thirty minutes a day from heavy usage experience lower levels of loneliness and depression and felt overall better after just three weeks.[21]

In the journal *Psychological Science* in 2016, a study found that the parts of our brain activated when eating chocolate or winning money are activated when teens see likes on their photos or their friends' photos.

In talking about the implications of this reality, Dr. Anastasiou from the study said:

> When we receive online "likes," the reward center of the brain, called the nucleus accumbens, lights up. With excessive use, this type of interaction can train the brain to release rewarding chemicals such as dopamine much the same way that addiction works with things like drugs, shopping, and gambling . . . This is worrisome because the more that someone uses social media, [the more] they come to expect and require this type of effect in order to feel happy.[23]

Self-Awareness

We need to look no further than our own lives to see the negative effects of social media.

For your own edification, how many minutes or hours do you wish you spent on social media a day, or a week? Take a quick look at your app usage. How many minutes or hours do you actually spend on media platforms?

Where is media adding value to your life currently? And in what ways is media having a negative impact on you?

How is media affecting your stress and anxiety levels? How is media breeding comparison? Is media keeping you from the real world, like time with your spouse, with your children, or with your community?

Is your media consumption affecting your ability to get to sleep when you'd prefer?

The goal in crafting intentionality truly is knowing yourself, your tendencies, your desires, and your goals and simply putting media in its proper place.

Like I've already said, you should only feel the trellis you've built when you start to pull away from it too far. It should provide tension to pull you back toward your intended desires and goals rather than restrict you from those things that will produce an abundant life.

A Personal Experience

A few years ago, I made the decision to delete my social media accounts and mostly disengage from social media companies. Knowing myself, I just wasn't able to craft a healthy relationship with these addictive platforms with any access or experience with them.

I didn't like the pull to pick up my phone whenever I had a quiet moment. I didn't like the comparison I felt scrolling through the feeds of people I wanted to emulate. I didn't like the question of whether or not I should be taking photos or videos of my experiences instead of being fully present in the moment.

My wife, however, genuinely cultivates meaningful relationships through social media. She loves staying connected with her friends and family and loves sharing the hilarious things our kids do, and it mostly adds positive meaning and interaction to her life.

With other media, I seek to limit my news consumption in the morning and limit television and movies in the evening and weekends so they don't interfere with my time alone with God or my rhythms before sleep.

Setting alarms can be incredibly helpful if you want to give only a certain portion of your time and attention to media. Sometimes, an audible reminder that your time is up can help you make the decision to exit what can be an addictive experience.

The point is, all of us are wired differently. In aggregate, modern media seems to be creating a fair amount of harm, but your decisions don't need to be made based on the aggregate.

I believe it's helpful to have caution when it comes to media, to use media for *your* purposes rather than be used for *its* purposes.

But as you venture into creating a rule for your media consumption, I want to encourage you to do so out of passion and desire rather than fear or doubt.

Take an honest look at your media consumption habits. Think about the positive and negative effects. Think and pray about what you want out of life, and what you feel most called to.

With courage, choose to create an intentionality that will most help you take hold of the good and leave behind the bad of media consumption.

Crafting a Rule for Media Consumption

———————— Guided Prayer: ————————

1. Take a moment to receive God's grace. Receive the mercy of God, that any leadership he provides is always joined with forgiveness, unconditional love, and sincere hope.

2. Take a moment to think about your current media consumption and to lay your current reality at the feet of Christ. Christ understands what it is to live in this world. Take time to rest in his presence.

3. Ask the Spirit to illuminate clearly and gently a pathway into a healthy relationship with media consumption. God's intention for our life is both peaceful and clear, kind and at times convicting. Commit to follow wherever it is he would lead.

———————— Guided Reflection: ————————

1. How do you feel about the current state of media? What do you like about media today? What do you not like? What do you find fulfilling or meaningful? What do you find unfulfilling?

_____

_____

_____

_____

2. Take some time to research your current media consumption. Go back through the last week or so and think about how much media you've consumed. Write out the main platforms you've used and how much time you've spent on them. If it's mobile applications, your phone should be able to tell you. If it's television or another type of media, make your best guess.

_____

_____

_____

_____

3. In what ways does your media consumption feel intentional already? Where do you feel like you're already in a healthy place related to your media consumption?

_____

_____

_____

_____

_____

4. What would you like your media consumption to look like? What platforms do you want to engage in, and for how long?

_____

_____

_____

_____

5. Where is there a gap between your desire and reality? Where are you spending too long consuming media in comparison to your desire? What else do you notice about the gap between your desire and reality?

_____

_____

_____

_____

6. Does simply noting how long you'd like to spend consuming media feel like enough intentionality? Do you need to limit the number of platforms you're on? Do you need to delete some accounts altogether? Do you need to implement a tool to limit your screen usage?

_____

_____

_____

_____

_____

7. Beyond platforms and time, are there any aspects within media platforms you need to change to have a more meaningful experience in life? Are there people you need to unfollow? Are there people you need to hide your content from? Are there any social media practices you need to change, such as engaging in arguments or scrolling without communicating?

_____

_____

_____

_____

8. Is there anyone you want to share your reflections and decisions with? Would your intentionality affect someone, such as a spouse, child, social media friend, or roommate? Rather than seeking to live with new intentionality on your own, it can be really helpful to communicate new goals or boundaries with people our changes in behaviors and actions will affect.

_____

_____

_____

_____

(Loose) Decisions:

I'm choosing to spend _____ minutes/hours a day on media consumption.

My goals in media consumption are to _____.

I am choosing to set up the following precautions in order to ensure I use media as a tool for my own purposes: _____.

Suggested Practices:

Set an alarm. Media platforms are too addictive to engage in them without a plan for disengaging. Setting an alarm can serve as an audible reminder to spend only as long as we intend consuming media.

Curate your own experience. Instead of allowing media platforms to curate your experience with more and more suggested content, only engage with those people and those shows that are sincerely meaningful for you. If you notice a media platform consistently pulling you into meaningless content, or even inciting anger or outrage in your mind and heart, make changes with what content you see on those platforms.

Leave your phone far from your bed or outside of your room. It can be too tempting to begin your day with media and end your day with media, and those rhythms make it really difficult to start and end your day meaningfully. Get a true alarm clock and choose to leave your phone away from your bed.

Chapter 7

Activity

❧

"We cannot do great things on this earth, only small things with great love."

—Mother Theresa

Whereas our world and often our faith communities prioritize a life of activity over a life of interior abundance, I believe Scripture, the Spirit, and our lived experience reverse this order of priority.

God doesn't need us. He doesn't need our intellect. He doesn't need our communication. He doesn't need our activity. Rather, on the basis of a thriving inward life, he invites us to join him in meaningful activity that's saturated in love.

John 15:5 says:

"I am the vine; you are the branches. Whoever abides in me and I in him, he it is that bears much fruit, for apart from me you can do nothing."

Jesus isn't saying that apart from abiding in him, we can't have a lot of activity. Jesus isn't saying that unless we abide in him, we won't be busy. What he is saying is that unless our activity comes from a place of genuinely abiding in him, our activity will not bear fruit.

To abide in work is to cease doing it on your own, in your own strength, and instead to fuel your activity from a place of spiritual connection, genuine health, and life-giving humility.

In America, we love the notion of independence. We love stories of the self-made man or woman. We love the idea that in our own strength, with enough hard work and tenacity, we can do anything. But in reality, those are not the principles of heaven.

God says that it is in our weakness that we invite his strength (2 Cor. 12:2). God says that it is the poor in spirit who will inherit the kingdom of heaven (Matt. 5:3). God says that it is those who lose their life in him who will find it (Matt. 10:39). God says that it is in taking up our cross that we are resurrected into heavenly eternal meaning and impact (Matt. 16:24–26).

That doesn't mean God doesn't have a unique and important calling for your life. He absolutely does.

Ephesians 2:10 says, *"For we are his workmanship, created in*

Christ Jesus for good works, which God prepared beforehand, that we should walk in them."

You were brought into this world at this exact time, in this exact place, for a reason.

But engaging in that work is not an obligation—it's an invitation. God does not need our work; he simply wants to do it with you. The kingdom of God doesn't need us to deepen its vibrancy in our world, but it invites us into that work for God's glory and our good.

A Life without Work

Scripture is also clear that if our life isn't producing fruit, if we aren't engaged in meaningful activity, there is something broken in our abiding connection with God.

A branch does not force fruit. Rather, it maintains its connection to a healthy, resource-giving vine, and naturally it bears fruit in its season.

If a branch isn't bearing fruit, something is wrong with its connection to the vine. Something is wrong with its health.

James 2:26 says, *"For as the body apart from the spirit is dead, so also faith apart from works is dead."*

The point of these sentiments isn't to try to kick you into gear. The point is that something is wrong, something is unhealthy, something needs an intentional investment if you are not engaging in meaningful activity.

There are absolutely times to simply follow through on a commitment to love others in obedience, even if desire is lacking.

But if overall you're exhausted, if overall you're unmotivated, if overall you're insecure, unhealthy, disconnected, and unproductive, then it's time to take a step back with God and revisit your health.

Consistently forcing fruit is the recipe for burnout. If you're struggling to authentically and naturally bear fruit, the goal is to figure out why with grace and gentleness.

Why don't you feel love toward others, even an enemy as God asks us? Where are you overcommitted? Where are you under-inspired?

It could be as simple as needing more time to recover from your activity. It could be as complex as engaging in a holistic assessment and rediscovery of your health and purpose.

Do not let forced activity go for too long without checking into the reason for a lack of authentic motivation and productivity.

The world doesn't need your forced activity. What it needs is the supernatural impact that comes from fruit born from a place of abiding in God and being saturated in his love.

Activity and Money

It seems in the last fifty years or so of theological exploration, we're finally beginning to engage with the false separation of the "clergy" and the "laity," finally taking steps to close the wrongful divide between the sacred and the secular.

Vocational ministry is not a "higher calling." Those who provide for themselves and their families through what we typically think of as vocational work do not by default have a clearer or closer connection with God.

Every believer—whether their work is in business, in government, in nonprofit work, in the home, in a church, or even if they're out of work—is a minister.

Ephesians 4:11–12 makes it clear that God has given *"the apostles, the prophets, the evangelists, the shepherds and teachers, to **equip the saints for the work of ministry** [emphasis mine], for building up the body of Christ."*

Those who have said yes to a vocational call do so for the equipping of God's people *"for the work of ministry."*

You have a ministry. Every day you have ample, perfect opportunities to bring God's kingdom to earth, to love those around you with the unconditional, present love of God.

You have the same Spirit as St. Paul, St. John, St. Teresa of Ávila, J. R. R. Tolkien, Dietrich Bonhoeffer, Martin Luther King, and C. S. Lewis.

You have a unique and needed call wherever God provides for you financially. But it's vital to remember that money is not our ultimate aim. God provides for each of us with a plan in mind for how we utilize those resources.

That doesn't mean God doesn't want you to own a home, even a nice home. He might have that for you. He might not.

That doesn't mean God doesn't want you to have possessions, to save, to invest, to be generous with your family and friends. He might have that for you. He might not.

The point is that money is not the point. It is a means to an end—hopefully a beautiful and lifegiving end.

In the days that money seems to be your aim, bring that realization to God, recognizing these words of caution from Paul:

"For the love of money is a root of all kinds of evils. It is through this craving that some have wandered away from the faith and pierced themselves with many pangs" (1 Tim. 6:10 NIV).

And as you lay down a pursuit of money, pick up the opportunity to store your treasure in heaven that your life might be filled with the fullness of heaven's joy (Matt. 6:21).

Unpaid Activity

As soaked up as our capacities can become from activity that generates financial provision, we need to recognize that often the activity that brings about the most impact and the most joy has absolutely nothing to do with money.

More than our children need money, they need our attention, our affection, our time, and our care.

More than our marriages need the money our jobs provide, they need meaningful conversation, vulnerability, and emotional support.

More than our churches need our financial support (even if that's what you get asked for most often), they need our passion, our capacities, and our willingness to invest our time and capacities in developing lasting relationships.

Remember, God does not need our money. Everything in this world is ultimately his. Instead, he invites us to give of ourselves to his kingdom totally and completely, money included.

Where do you need to generate a healthier balance with work to make space for the unpaid activity that is so vital to living an intentionally meaningful life?

Spontaneous Activity

Finally, one of the hardest forms of activity for me to make space for is spontaneous activity. I love having a plan. And I hate interruptions.

Most of the time, my head is in the clouds and I hardly see or notice the world that's happening right in front of me.

Unless we make space for the spontaneous activity God might have for us moment to moment, we can miss out on some of the most vibrant experiences this life has to offer, as well as some of the greatest opportunities to love our neighbor.

Are you too busy to say yes to your child's desire to crawl up into your lap for a few moments?

Are you too busy cooking, cleaning, budgeting, consuming media, or conversing with friends to be available and attentive to the pull to solitude, to family, to a tug from the Spirit?

Are your commitments so critical, or your mind so distracted, that you don't have space to help a stranger in need?

Unless we establish room for spontaneity in our lives, we'll never find the abundant life that God wants to surprise us with.

A Quick Test

If you're wondering if you're in a healthy, intentional relationship with activity in your life, there are a few sentiments of Scripture that can help you find the answer.

The first sentiment is a sense of ease in our activity. Matthew 11:28–30 says:

> *"Come to me, all who labor and are heavy laden, and I will give you rest. Take my yoke upon you, and learn from me, for I am gentle and lowly in heart, and you will find rest for your souls. For my yoke is easy, and my burden is light."*

The moment we lose a sense of ease about the activity God has invited us into, we can know that we have put too much responsibility on our own shoulders.

Ultimately, this world is God's. Ultimately, the kingdom of heaven is God's. Ultimately, God is pursuing and drawing to himself every person known by us and unknown by us.

We are simply invited into the joy and meaningful purpose of joining with him in reflecting his glory and nature and being a representative of his unceasing devotion and love for his creation.

You are enough for this work God has called you to.

The second sentiment is the fruit of the Spirit's presence and saturation in our lives. Galatians 5:22–23 says:

> *But the fruit of the Spirit is love, joy, peace, patience, kindness, goodness, faithfulness, gentleness, self-control.*

Unless our activity is marked by this sort of fruit, then we are not allowing the Spirit to anoint and saturate our activity.

All that God does is marked by these types of experiences. And it's vital to take time as we engage in activity to ensure our activity is exhibiting this fruit.

Remember that activity, if not done from a place of abiding connection, if not filled with the life of God, will not produce fruit that matters.

Intentional Activity

On the basis of abiding connection, with acknowledgment that ultimately all our activity, whether paid, unpaid, or spontaneous, is kingdom activity, we can create a sense of intentionality about those parts of our lives that are most visible.

Remember that as you craft a rule for your activity, too much activity will be good for no one, least of all you.

With so much opportunity for activity, and in living in a world that defines us by what we do more than who we are, our lives will need to look more focused and less active than many of those we're surrounded by.

Thus, craft a rule for your activity that works for you, for this season you're in. And know that if, or when, you fail to live by your intentional goal, whether it's by too much or too little activity, the goal is to fail forward every day by God's grace.

Crafting a Rule for Activity

1. Begin with stillness. Psalm 46:10 says, *"Be still, and know that I am God. I will be exalted among the nations, I will be exalted in the earth!"* Acknowledge that no matter what you do, God will be exalted. The weight of his kingdom and this world is not on your shoulders.

2. Meditate on the nature of authentic activity. Think about the ease of working yoked to God, about the fruit of the Spirit, about being active from a place of inner flourishing.

3. Commit to engage in meaningful action. Reflect on the ease by which a healthy branch bears fruit. Seek to associate health with a natural ability to genuinely love others. Ask God for a revelation of what that could look like.

———————— Guided Reflection: ————————

1. How have you generally seen activity?
Does abundant activity come natural to you already? What's usually at the root of your activity? What sorts of things give you active energy the most?

_____

_____

_____

_____

_____

2. Where might God be inviting you to redefine activity?
Where do you sense an opportunity to change the way you
view and engage in meaningful activity?

_____

_____

_____

_____

3. Do you see the whole of your activity as sacred?
Or do you divide your activity into categories, such as good
or bad, godly or worldly, sacred or secular?

_____

_____

_____

_____

**4. What do you want your relationship with paid activity to
look like?** Do you want to find a way to work more and earn
more? Do you need to find a better way to achieve balance
between your paid work and the rest of life? What might a
better relationship with paid work look like in this next season?

_____

_____

_____

_____

_____

5. What do you want your relationship with unpaid activity to look like? What sort of time do you want to commit to your community, hobbies, and other relationships?

_____

_____

_____

_____

6. What sort of space do you want to make for spontaneous activity? Do you need to carve out real room around your commitments, or does making space look more like a mental reframing of spontaneous activity? What do you think this might add to your life? What about it makes you nervous, if anything?

_____

_____

_____

_____

7. What needs to change in other areas of your life to facilitate meaningful, authentic, and energetic activity?

Where do you need to be less distracted or busy? What do you need to do to recover well from activity so you have more capacity each day?

_____

_____

_____

_____

_____

_____

8. Overall, does a more meaningful relationship with activity look like more recovery, less distraction, or a greater sense of purpose? If multiples of areas seem meaningful for the next season, seek to prioritize them so you can have a better intentional focus to make changes.

_____

_____

_____

_____

(Loose) Decisions:

Meaningful, paid action in this next season looks like

_____.

Meaningful, unpaid action in this next season looks like

_____.

Meaningful, spontaneous action in this next season looks like _____.

To facilitate more meaningful action, I am going to take these few steps: _____.

To recover from action, I am going to daily _____.

To recover from action, I am going to weekly _____.

To recover from action, I am going to annually _____.

Suggested Practices:

Find what helps you best recover. Different people receive energy in different ways, and a critical key to consistently engaging in meaningful action is recovery. Creating a plan for meaningful recovery before you reach exhaustion helps you continue enjoying the wonderful opportunities God gives you to bear visible fruit every day.

Engage in the discipline of solitude. Often, what we need to fuel loving activity is a break from all the stimulation. Finding just ten minutes a day when you can close your eyes, focus on your breath, and rest in the presence of God free from thought, stimulation, or activity can do wonders for your ability to engage in action. If you're feeling burnt out or tired, try ten minutes of solitude.

Work in your natural uniqueness. God doesn't always call us to activity we feel especially wired for or naturally gifted at. But in general, I believe God wants us to work in our strengths. If God's calling is stretching you, say yes to that. But if you are continually operating outside of what energizes you and what you feel equipped for, it might be time to reassess better areas for your activity.

Chapter 8

Generosity

∽

"It takes generosity to discover the whole through others. If you realize you are only a violin, you can open yourself up to the world by playing your role in the concert."

—Jacques-Yves Cousteau

A Case for Generosity

Many of the truths of Jesus's teachings are rooted in the paradoxical reality that our quality of life is directly connected to our generosity.

Luke 6:37–38 says:

"Judge not, and you will not be judged; condemn not, and you will not be condemned; forgive, and you will be forgiven; give, and it will be given to you. Good measure, pressed down, shaken together, running over, will be put into your lap. For with the measure you use it will be measured back to you."

Jesus says here that our experiences of judgment, of forgiveness, and of receiving are directly tied to our generosity. Somehow, when we freely give away our time, talent, and treasure, we position ourselves to receive more freely.

In relationships, when we're willing to be generous with our time, generous with our vulnerability, generous with our words, and generous with our assumptions, we find that opens the path for others to reciprocate.

Scripture also speaks directly to the reciprocal effects of generosity as it relates to our finances and resources:

One gives freely, yet grows all the richer; another withholds what he should give, and only suffers want. Whoever brings blessing will be enriched, and one who waters will himself be watered" (Proverbs 11:24–25).

If we are to build a trellis for our lives, a system that produces the quality of life I believe we're all striving for, that trellis has to provide intentionality as it relates to our generosity.

The Nature of Our Generosity

To be clear, the joy of generosity does not come from expectation of what we'll get in return. And the worth of our generosity isn't linked to the number of earthly resources we have and are therefore able to give away.

God does not need one bit of our resources. Every resource is his. As in all things with God, the main point of generosity is not the possession, but the heart of the giver.

God cares about the nature of how we view our treasure because he cares about the affinity of our hearts:

"For where your treasure is, there your heart will be also" (Matt: 6:21).

God knows the hold our resources can have on us. He knows the toll it takes when we hoard that which he's given us. Because when we hoard our resources in this life, we miss the entirety of the point of why we're here.

This world is not our home. This life—while beautiful and wonderful and filled with the possibility of relationships and meaningful experiences—pales in comparison to what eternity holds for us.

We have been given through relationship with an eternal God an eternal opportunity to live without fear of lack now. We're invited to say yes to an eternal mindset now and to experience the heavenly joy of God's economy where all is given by grace.

A beautiful picture of God's view of generosity is found in the experience of Jesus with a widow in Mark 12:41–44:

And he sat down opposite the treasury and watched the people putting money into the offering box. Many rich people put in large sums. And a poor widow came and put in two small copper coins, which make a penny. And he called his disciples to him and said to them, "Truly, I say to you, this poor widow has put in more than all those who are contributing to the offering box. For they all contributed out of their abundance, but she out of her poverty has put in everything she had, all she had to live on."

In God's economy, the nature of our generosity is not defined by how much we give, but by how much we have left.

Three Lenses of Generosity
When thinking about generosity, I've found it to be most helpful to look at my resources through three different lenses: time, talent, and treasure.

God is not after your money. He's after your heart. (FYI: I'm probably going to keep saying this just to be sure it hits home.)

God hasn't just given you money as a resource to be generous with. He's uniquely wired you as a part of his body. He's given you time here on this earth that you can freely give away in meaningful conversation, with loving attention, in being there for others in times of celebration and times of need.

What God invites us into is a holistic opportunity to give ourselves away as he does, that we might discover the immense joy that's found in interdependence over self-sufficiency.

Time

Rick Warren said, "The best use of life is love. The best expression of love is time. The best time to love is now."

The one resource in a given day that we all share equally is time. And the older I get, the more I realize that time, more than money, might be the most valuable thing I have to offer to both God and others. I've heard it said that the best ability is availability.

We can be immensely talented. We can be highly affluent. We can be emotionally and intellectually intelligent in uncommonly gifted ways.

But it is in our generosity of time, simply being present with those around us, that life's greatest experience—truly meaningful relationship—is developed.

No marriage can thrive without time spent communicating and connecting, regardless of the possessions a family might have.

No family can thrive without the parents and children spending quality time together experiencing the joy of a meaningful relationship.

Our relationship with God does not flourish on the basis of our activity and giving, even when done so in service to God's kingdom. God is after our hearts, and activity and giving are meant to express the love we've cultivated through quality time together.

As you craft intentionality around your time, seek to create space for what matters most. As much as the needs of the day might feel highly urgent, you must protect your calendar so that you can spend large amounts of quality time with those God has given you to cultivate relationships with the most.

Talent

You are talented. No matter what the world has told you about yourself. No matter what you believe about yourself. God has made you, fearfully and wonderfully, with a unique wiring, purpose, and calling in this earth (Ps. 139:14).

You have a valuable place in the body of Christ. You were born for a valuable contribution in this exact moment in our world.

Maybe some of your talents reside in those areas this world typically admires, and you don't need a reminder that you're talented. If so, just remember to focus those talents on areas of God's calling that might not produce results—such as monetary gain or status—that this world values most.

Maybe your talents don't reside in areas this world normally admires. Maybe you haven't achieved status, or wealth, or visibility. Maybe your more passive talents—such as wonder, or discernment, or empathy, those things about you that feel more under the surface or invisible—haven't been called beautiful and necessary.

For each of us, every day is an opportunity to bring who we uniquely are to its fullest expression for God's glory and our good. And to do so, we need intentionality.

We need to look for opportunities to share our talents with others, whether or not that results in financial gain or celebrated societal benefit.

We need to steward and cultivate our talents, to grow in awareness and maximization of those ways God has wired us so he can use our talents to their greatest potential.

As you craft a rule for generosity, think through how you can be generous with your wiring, with your uniqueness, and with God's anointing on your life. Instead of seeking to conserve it, vulnerably give it away with a confidence and strength that comes only from a secure sense of your identity in God.

Treasure

Finally, it's critical that we are generous with our treasure. Every dollar you have was given to you for a purpose. No matter how hard you have worked, your work is merely a "yes" to God's invitation for provision, because everything you have has been given by God's grace alone.

You did not have to be born where you were born. You did not have to have the parents you had, the education, the friends, the opportunities, all the things that have helped you acquire the resources you have right now.

And in generously giving of our treasure, we find a joy that cannot be found in material possessions. In freely giving away our finances, we get to experience a part of the joy God feels when he provides for us as his children. We get to join in the care for others, the care for this earth, and the opportunity for God's kingdom to radically transform the hearts and minds and lives of those who need transformation the most.

But 2 Corinthians 9:7 also cautions us, *"Each one must give as he has decided in his heart, not reluctantly or under compulsion, for God loves a cheerful giver."*

Again, God is not after your money. God is after your heart.

When we generously give of our finances, with the joy that comes from releasing our hearts from the frivolous pursuit of the temporal, we find a higher and deeper joy that comes from giving our hearts to the eternal.

To create a Rule of Life that has the most profound impact on our quality of life, that system of intentionality must contain a plan for generously giving of our finances.

As you create your plan, pay attention to those areas where you feel pause. Pay attention to reasons why it's hard or exciting to think about giving your finances.

Think about those things you would most like to give to, those passions you would feel immense joy in seeing made better as a result of your generosity.

The only wrong choice when it comes to where you invest your finances is choosing to give nothing at all.

Crafting a Rule for Generosity

——————————— Guided Prayer: ———————————

1. Take a moment to meditate on God's call to be generous.
Second Corinthians 9:6 says, *"Whoever sows sparingly will also reap sparingly, and whoever sows bountifully will also reap bountifully."* Take time for these words to sink from your head to your heart in prayer.

2. Ask the Holy Spirit for inspiration around your generosity. Ask him to illuminate the current posture of your heart. Where do you feel a temptation to hoard? Where are you looking for deep satisfaction from that which can never fully satisfy you?

3. Commit to engaging in joyful generosity. Commit to following wherever God would lead you in trust that God has true, abundant life in saying yes to his invitation to generosity.

———————— Guided Reflection: ————————

1. What does generosity look like for you now?
What parts of generosity come easy for you? What parts of generosity are more difficult? What do you feel like you currently give away freely versus having a temptation to waste or keep?

_____

_____

_____

_____

2. What did generosity look like in your family when you were growing up? Did you see your parents be generous with their time, talent, or treasure? Did you give as a family? How might your family of origin have impacted your sense of what is good or normal?

_____

_____

_____

_____

3. What would you like generosity with your time to look like in the next season? What would it look like to create space to give your time away more freely to your family, your friends, to needs or opportunities you see around you?

_____

_____

_____

_____

4. What would you like generosity with your talents to look like in the next season? How could you make some space week to week to share your skills with those who could benefit from them? Where can you volunteer? Who can you mentor?

_____

_____

_____

_____

5. What would you like generosity with your treasure to look like in the next season? What would bring you immense joy for you to invest your finances in? What transformation would you like to see in the world?

_____

_____

_____

_____

_____

6. What needs to change in your perspective currently to allow for a greater joy in generosity? Where could you take time to read or study to gain a new perspective? Who could you ask to mentor you to learn from?

_____

_____

_____

_____

_____

7. What needs to change practically in your life to make more space for generosity? Where do you need to engage in better stewardship so you have more capacity to give? What changes can you make so you have more time, more energy, and more finances to invest?

_____

_____

_____

_____

_____

8. How could you see a step forward in generosity in the next season positively impacting your life the most?
How could a consistent experience of generosity help facilitate the intentional, meaningful life you're hoping for?

_____

_____

_____

_____

(Loose) Decisions:

I'd like for generosity with my time in this next season to look like _____.

I'd like for generosity with my talent in this next season to look like _____.

I'd like for generosity with my treasure in this next season to look like _____.

To grow my perspective on generosity in this next season, I will _____.

To steward my capacity for generosity in this next season, I will _____.

Suggested Practices:

Plan your generosity with your family. It's easier and more joyful to engage in generosity with others around you doing the same. Whether it's creating room for your time, talents, or treasure, it's immensely helpful to do that in agreement with your family.

Have a weekly holistic budget meeting. Don't just review your finances; determine how you're spending your time and energy as well. Taking an honest look at your past week, celebrating the victories of intentionality, and acknowledging with grace areas of improvement is a helpful catalyst for generosity and intentionality in the week to come.

Do an annual study of generosity. There are lots of great resources, conferences, and guides for generosity. Studying stewardship, giving, and best practices can serve as a great reminder and help you find the highest impact for your "yes" to be generous.

Closing

"Almighty God, give me wisdom to perceive You, intelligence to understand You, diligence to seek You, patience to wait for You, eyes to behold You, a heart to meditate upon You and life to proclaim You, through the power of the Spirit of our Lord Jesus Christ. Amen."

—Benedict of Nursia

When I walked through this process myself, I felt both excited and overwhelmed. You may be feeling that way too.

Making intentional changes to every area of life isn't easy. But the prospect of finding more meaning, purpose, and fulfillment in every area of life is incredibly exciting.

The pathway from here, in my opinion, looks simply like practicing these decisions with utter grace.

New Mercies

Across this next season, cling to the promise of Lamentations 3:22–23:

> *"The steadfast love of the LORD never ceases; his mercies never come to an end; they are new every morning; great is your faithfulness."*

No matter how well you implement these decisions, God's love for you is steadfast. You have a whole lifetime to live more and more intentionally. And it's often in our failure that we learn life's most profound lessons.

Just don't give up. Try one new thing at a time—whatever decision feels most meaningful for you. Be honest about whether your practices are working. And every day keep working toward intentionality.

One Key

If there's one thing you can do that can serve as a key to unlocking the rest of your plan for intentionality, it's to spend meaningful time alone with God first thing every day.

If, first thing every morning, you will set aside your phone, wake up before your family, choose not to engage in work, and spend meaningful time in the presence of God, you'll find that choice far easier in every other aspect of your day.

Beginning your day with self-assessment, with centering your life on God's character in worship, with engaging your heart and mind with Scripture and reading, and reminding yourself of the open pathway for communication with God in prayer will have a massive effect on your ability to live meaningfully throughout your day.

In even fifteen minutes, you can have a transformative experience with God every morning.

More Resources

For more resources on a Rule of Life and other aspects of living an intentional, vibrant life with God, check out First15.org where we have daily devotionals, books, blogs, conversations, and more.

We're here to help you close the gap between your desire for God and a fruitful life with him and to see that desire come to fruition every day.

Acknowledgments

Tireless heart, passion, and effort from so many went into the creation of this guide to greater intentionality.

I first want to thank those who have gone before us in the creation of rhythms such as a Rule of Life. St. Benedict's Rule of Life has meant so much for so many. I'm especially grateful for modern communities and communicators and writers such as Pete Scazzero and New Life Fellowship, John Mark Comer and Bridgetown Church, and Margaret Guenther and her book, *At Home in the World: A Rule of Life for the Rest of Us*. Without their wisdom, spiritual maturity, and gifted communication, I would have never discovered this framework for myself or created this guide for others.

Thank you to my wife Rachel, who has always been the first set of eyes on everything I've written. Because of your kindness, support, and giftings, my often nebulous ideas become concrete and, therefore, actually meaningful for others.

Thank you to Josh Miller, who truly leads everything related to First15. Your humility, creativity, and flexibility have made this resource and countless others possible.

Thank you to my parents, Jim and Janet Denison, for modeling an authentic faith while also communicating the goodness and glory of God to the masses. Too few Christian leaders match their words with their lives, and I am forever grateful to you.

Thank you to my team of gifted leaders of Denison Ministries: Jeff, Jen, Matt, Alex, and Krista. Because of your giftedness, I was able to create the space needed to write this resource. It is one of my greatest joys to work alongside you all.

And last, thank you to my boys, Wesley and Wells, who show me every day exactly why I so desperately want to live my life intentionally. Every moment with you is saturated with joy and love, and I wish to spend as many moments with you as possible.

Notes

ONE—Unintentional Consequences

1. "The Rule of Saint Benedict," The Rule, Friends of Saint Benedict, accessed November 11, 2020, http://www.benedictfriend.org/the-rule.html.

TWO—A Rule of Life

2. Margaret Guenther, *At Home in the World: A Rule of Life for the Rest of Us* (New York: Church Publishing Incorporated, 2006), 13.
3. "How do I choose an appropriate trellis system for my vineyard?" Posts, Grapes, last modified June 20, 2019, https://grapes.extension.org/how-do-i-choose-an-appropriate-trellis-system-for-my-vineyard/.
4. Guenther, 11.
5. "Adult Obesity Facts," Data & Statistics, Overweight & Obesity, CDC, last modified June 29, 2020, https://www.cdc.gov/obesity/data/adult.html.

THREE—An Overarching Goal

6. Saint Augustine, *Homilies on the First Epistle of John* (Hyde Park, New York: New City Press, 2008), 110.

FIVE—Health

7. John F. Kennedy, "The Soft American," *Sports Illustrated*, December 26, 1960, http://www.recreatingwithkids.com/news/read-it-here-kennedys-the-soft-american/.
8. "Benefits of Physical Activity," Physical Activity Basics, Physical Activity, CDC, last modified October 7, 2020, https://www.cdc.gov/physicalactivity/basics/pa-health/index.htm.
9. CDC, "Benefits of Physical Activity."
10. CDC, "Benefits of Physical Activity."
11. CDC, "Adult Obesity Facts."
12. CDC, "Adult Obesity Facts."
13. "Short Sleep Duration Among US Adults," Data & Statistics, Sleep, Centers for Disease Control and Prevention, last modified May 2, 2017, https://www.cdc.gov/sleep/data_statistics.html.

SIX—Relationships

14. "Social Media Use and Perceived Social Isolation Among Young Adult in the US," American Journal of Preventative Medicine, March 6, 2017, https://www.ajpmonline.org/article/S0749-3797(17)30016-8/fulltext.

SEVEN—Media Consumption

15. Vaughan Bell, "Don't Touch That Dial!" *Slate*, February 15, 2010, https://slate.com/technology/2010/02/a-history-of-media-technology-scares-from-the-printing-press-to-facebook.html.
16. Bell, "Don't Touch That Dial!"
17. Walter Karp, "Where the Media Critics Went Wrong," *American*

Heritage, accessed December 3, 2020, https://www.americanheritage. com/where-media-critics-went-wrong.

18. Sabrina Barr, "Six Ways Social Media Negatively Affects Your Mental Health," *Independent*, October 7, 2020, https://www. independent.co.uk/life-style/health-and-families/social-media- mental-health-negative-effects-depression-anxiety-addiction- memory-a8307196.html.

19. "2019 Modern Wealth Survey," Charles Schwab, accessed December 3, 2020, https://www.aboutschwab.com/modernwealth2019.

20. Keith Wilcox, Andrew T. Stephen, "Are Close Friends the Enemy? Online Social Networks, Self-Esteem, and Self-Control," Journal of Consumer Research, November 27, 2012, https://academic.oup.com/jcr/article/40/1/90/1792313.

21. Mai-Ly N. Steers, Robert E. Wickham, Linda K. Acitelli, "Seeing Everyone Else's Highlight Reels: How Facebook Usage is Linked to Depressive Symptoms," Journal of Social and Clinical Psychology, accessed December 3, 2020, https://guilfordjournals.com/doi/ abs/10.1521/jscp.2014.33.8.70.

22. Steers, Wickham, Acitelli, "How Facebook Usage is Linked to Depressive Symptoms."

23. Damon Beres, "10 Negative Effects of Social Media on Your Brain," *The Healthy*, updated November 12, 2020, https://www.thehealthy. com/mental-health/negative-effects-of-social-media/.

About the Author

Craig Denison is the CEO of Denison Ministries and author of First15, a daily devotional guiding over a million believers into a fresh experience with God's presence every day. He writes and speaks, and he and his wife Rachel lead worship to help believers establish a more tangible, meaningful connection with God. Craig and Rachel live in Dallas, Texas, with their two sons. You can check out his devotional work by signing up to receive First15 every morning for free at First15.org and by engaging with First15 on social media. For more of Craig's resources, visit First15.org/store.

www.first15.org
Instagram: @first15devotional
contact@first15.org

Leave a Review

If you enjoyed *Living Intentionally*, will you consider leaving a review on your platform of choice? Reviews help authors find more readers like you.